A Welcoming Elegance

Suzanne Rheinstein
A WELCOMING ELEGANCE

PHOTOGRAPHY BY PIETER ESTERSOHN
WRITTEN BY MICHAEL BOODRO

RIZZOLI
NEW YORK

New York Paris London Milan

To my daughter, Kate, and to her daughters,
Beatriz, Frederica, and Delphine,
with so much affection and gratitude.

Table of Contents

Introduction

There is a saying in the design and architectural community, "Your work is only as good as your clients allow you to be." That refrain has become common because it is true.

I love all the houses in this book. Each of them was a real collaboration between designer and clients. All these clients came to me with rich lives and varying points of view about how they wanted to live and the possessions they already owned. Many were travelers with beautiful and meaningful treasures they had gathered along the way. Others were collectors who had assembled their art and objects over many years. What they all have in common is that each house tells a story and is very personal—unlike so many homes today, which decidedly are not. There was no tabula rasa here, no clean sweep, no starting over or throwing everything out.

Some of these clients have growing families, with in-laws and grandchildren. Others are empty nesters. All were in the process of adapting to changed circumstances, and we aimed to make that a comfortable transition, whether it was reimagining houses for couples who entertain graciously, making way for new babies joining the family, or in my own case, crafting a comfortable and cosseting place for me to be alone amid nature in Santa Barbara.

It can be challenging to work with the things that clients bring with them—challenging, yes, but also rewarding. I was fortunate that these clients had lived in wonderful houses and possessed interesting and compelling furniture and objects that held meaning for them. Together, we chose the pieces we would use, and shopped for new pieces that would fit in.

I am known for plunging into dusty warehouses with flashlights or to haunt magpie dealers with inventory piled in a series of warrens and rooms—I love the hunt! Nothing gives me more pleasure than finding one-of-a-kind pieces and offering them to happily surprised clients. And one-of-a-kind can mean anything from a beautifully worn wooden bowl to a gorgeous Carmen Almon tole botanical sculpture. To me, coming upon a fine old rattan chair is as exciting as finding a rare painted and gilded eighteenth-century Milanese console.

Resilience and flexibility are important in life (as well as in design). These houses are the last I plan to do, as I have closed my studio, and all the designers who worked with me at SRA have started their own businesses. While working on these projects, the storage warehouse we used burned down, and with that we lost not only specially bought antiques for clients, but also family treasures of theirs and of mine that had been placed into storage temporarily. The fire was devastating. But we all pulled ourselves together and got on with it.

The same is true with cancer, which I have been dealing with. Things happen. Good and not so good. But whatever happens, it is important to have a space to which you can retreat and in which you can feel comfortable and truly at home. Having beautiful things around you is wonderful but living beautifully is more important. All of us deserve a place that adds richness and serenity to our lives and that we can happily share with friends and family. Creating that kind of home for my clients has been my goal throughout my career in design.

—*Suzanne Rheinstein*

Northern California

OPENING SPREAD: The dramatic sweep of the staircase in the entry hall is emphasized by the compass rose on the floor and a monochromatic mural of trees that rises to the second floor, both painted by Bob Christian. The neoclassical settee and painted chairs are covered in a faded red mattress ticking. PRECEDING SPREAD: The new rear porch, added during the renovation by architect Mark Ferguson of Ferguson & Shamamian Architects, has become a favorite spot for the family to gather and enjoy the surrounding vineyards and old oak trees. RIGHT: The symmetry that is so important to the serene mood of the house is immediately evident in the entry hall where English chinoiserie painted chests topped with Regency gilt mirrors flank the archway and make a welcoming approach to the living room.

The adage goes, wherever you go, there you are. This is certainly true of the personal issues that we all carry with us, but it also applies to our history, our memories, our passions, and our tastes. So, it is perhaps not surprising that when a couple who had raised their family in a classic New England town relocated to the West Coast, they brought with them a love of traditional American architecture, and a desire to be surrounded by graceful proportions, high ceilings, and elegant detailing.

The husband and wife both loved the wild and beautiful landscape of Northern California and were excited by the possibility of engaging more directly with nature and restoring and maintaining a property there. They also had family and friends living in the region, which made the decision to head west easier. Yet the house they chose, a white-painted 1940s Georgian, is an anomaly in the area.

The house is located on an expansive property outside a small town that has retained its natural beauty, its feeling for the past, and many of its historic wood-framed structures. In fact, over the decades, the town has become so identified with dark, timbered buildings that local zoning no longer permits white houses, though

OPPOSITE: The entry's grand-scaled Dutch brass chandelier leads the eye up to the second-floor landing and a dramatic Chinese screen. FOLLOWING SPREAD: The living room's paneling, moldings, and mantel were painted in a silvery gray *faux bois*, a palette amplified by a design of softly colored leaves painted by Bob Christian. The clients already owned much of the furniture, including the antique tables and painted chairs. A custom coffee table of vivid blue lacquer reiterates and amplifies the blues in the upholstery fabrics, and an Italian bench parallels the curve of the bay window overlooking the pond and vineyard.

ABOVE AND OPPOSITE: Small banquettes upholstered in Rheinstein's Cambria Crewel for Lee Jofa flank the archway. On the walls, panels of antique Chinese wallpaper are interspersed with gilded mirrors of hand-rolled glass that softly reflect the scene. The painted chairs are Italian.

this one was grandfathered in. The couple had no intention of buying a property quite so large, but they loved the setting, bordered by a nature preserve, and they responded to the house and its echoes of the grand East Coast homes they were familiar with.

The place was hardly in move-in condition, however. The interior was lackluster, and the great old oak trees surrounding the house had suffered from fifty years of deferred maintenance. A designer in New York who had gone to college with the wife and designed the couple's Manhattan pied-à-terre suggested that they reach out to Rheinstein for help. And the architect the couple chose was Mark Ferguson of Ferguson & Shamamian Architects, whose work she admired.

"We all agreed we wanted to restore the house, to maintain what was there but make it better—snappy and shiny," the designer says. "We would look to the grace and proportions of late 1930s and '40s architecture, when the house was first built." That entailed tearing down a large but ungainly section and crafting a new wing that blended with the original architecture without imitating it. The house is now slightly smaller than before but is far more practical and graceful in its layout. A new covered back porch deepens the connection to the rugged landscape of grasses, grapevines, old oak trees, and small ponds, while a new side patio, shaded by a striped awning, is oriented toward the swimming pool, pergola, and croquet court, with the hills beyond.

Rheinstein sought to create rooms that would not feel formal, but gracious and relaxed, using many of the furniture pieces the couple already owned, a collection that had been shaped by the wife's youth in the South. The couple are both major readers

PRECEDING SPREAD AND OPPOSITE: A sisal rug in the dining room softens the formality of the handsome traditional furniture and crystal chandelier. The walls are adorned with a series of tree of life confections by Bob Christian that give the illusion of having been painted on panels of fabric. Their silvery tonality creates a lovely background for gatherings, especially in candlelight.

and both wanted to feel drawn into every room to read. Symmetry would be key, in both layout and furniture placement, to establish a visual rhythm that serves as a quiet backdrop for gatherings both intimate and lively. But that symmetry is broken up with a few dramatic gestures, such as the sweeping stair in the entry hall, so the rooms never become monotonous or expected.

The living room, with its expansive bay window overlooking a pond and a small vineyard, connects directly to the outdoors, and there was no reason to try to compete with that view. "This is, very deliberately, not a 'wow' room," Rheinstein says, "but rather a place of comfort and calm, with thoughtful details that reveal themselves slowly over time." The original wood moldings, paneling, and mantel contrasted harshly with the abundant sunlight, so her favorite decorative artist, Bob Christian, was brought in to paint them a slivery gray, sun-bleached *faux bois*. In addition to the sofas and the beautiful eighteenth-century painted side chairs, the couple also owned a collection of lovely Chinese wallpaper panels. "We were so fortunate they had those. We hung them around the room, interspersed with gilded mirrors of hand-rolled glass that give a lovely soft effect," she says. "I sold a great many iterations of those mirrors when I had my Los Angeles shop, Hollyhock."

An early nineteenth-century Italian bench perfectly parallels the curve of the bay window and provides an ideal place to perch during the couple's frequent parties and family get-togethers. A custom vivid blue lacquered coffee table reiterates the subtle notes of blue throughout. And all the elements are grounded by a simple sisal rug.

PRECEDING SPREAD: A small patio set amid the gravel makes an ideal spot for lunch, shaded by the property's old oak trees. OPPOSITE: In the passage between the dining room and library, a pair of settees is covered in a printed linen by Rosa Bernal; custom Hundi lamps of cranberry glass reiterate their splashes of red.

Sisal appears again in the dining room, lightening the formality of the traditional dining table and chairs. Here, Bob Christian painted the walls with a series of floral confections that look as if they have been executed on fabric hangings, evoking the seasons and the tree of life motif. Their silvery tonality creates a lovely background.

The library is a traditional room done in an untraditional color. The walls and ceiling are lacquered in the same vibrant, glossy green, a more saturated version of the greens in the living room, so that light seems to bounce around the room, like eternal spring.

In the expansive kitchen, the appliances were reconfigured and grouped together to create a more efficient layout for cooking and are set off with simple Shaker-inspired cabinetry. Checkerboard painted floors unify the spacious work area, pantry, and the breakfast table, which has stunning views of the hills.

The couple's bedroom is a bower of leaves and vines, thanks to walls covered in a hand-blocked linen installed on the reverse side to create a soft effect. "This is one of my favorite techniques," Rheinstein says, "and can only be done with real hand-blocked fabrics—with machine-printed fabrics, the ink doesn't go all the way through. In fact, I designed my Garden Roses fabric, which we used in a guest room, to look as if it is the 'wrong' side."

One of the most popular spots in the house is the new back porch. Here, protected from the sun, the couple, often joined by family and friends, gather to admire the dramatic landscape that was, after all, one of the reasons for their move, even as they are sheltered and cossetted in a house that reflects and celebrates all that they left behind.

OPPOSITE: The powder room is a chinoiserie fantasy, with walls and vanity festooned by Bob Christian with magical flora, fauna, and trees. He also fashioned the setting for the hand-rolled mirror, transforming it into a tiny pagoda.

RIGHT: The walls, ceiling, and mantel in the library are lacquered the same vibrant green—Benjamin Moore's Herb Garden—so that light seems to bounce around the room. The sofa is covered in Rheinstein's Lanare Paisley, and the tufted ottoman is upholstered in a pale gray nubuck, inset with green leather buttons. On either side of the fireplace are an Italian inlaid table and an armchair covered in a woven stripe of wool and linen that is also used for the curtains.

RIGHT: The kitchen was reconfigured to create a more welcoming layout. Several shades of green were used on the cabinets and floor, mainly Farrow & Ball's Calke Green and Benjamin Moore's Yorktowne Green. The matching pendant lights are by the Urban Electric Company.

ABOVE AND OPPOSITE: Checkerboard painted floors unify the spacious work area, pantry, and breakfast nook, which has stunning views of the hills. The chairs are upholstered in Rheinstein's Indian Zag fabric.

RIGHT. On the second-floor landing, the Chinese screen sets off the graceful lines of an English Regency console. The chairs are English Regency, japanned with gilt detailing.

ABOVE: The hallway leading to the primary bedroom is painted in Farrow & Ball's Oval Room Blue. The Italian chest is eighteenth century and decoupaged with flowers from a silk textile. OPPOSITE AND FOLLOWING SPREAD: The primary bedroom is a bower of leaves and vines, thanks to walls covered in hand-blocked Lee Jofa linen installed on the reverse side to create a softer effect. The sleigh bed was upholstered in a gray-green velvet, and the *duchesse brisée* is covered in an embroidered cotton. Soft wall-to-wall carpeting, plush seating, and plenty of books add to the comfort.

RIGHT: The walls of a guest room are covered in Rheinstein's Garden Roses fabric, which was designed to look as if it were being used on the wrong side. The pen-and-ink drawings above the bed are by Rachel Lee Hovnanian. FOLLOWING SPREAD: The second floor of the porch, off the stair landing, provides an ideal view of the oval lawn and vineyard beyond.

RIGHT: Protected from the sun under a ceiling painted in Benjamin Moore's Palladian Blue, family and friends can gather to admire the dramatic landscape that originally attracted the clients to the property. FOLLOWING SPREAD: A new pergola with classic teak furniture provides shade and shelter at the pool.

50

West Hollywood

For many people, the word "retreat" conjures images of a secluded beach house, a remote farmhouse, a ski chalet high amid snowy peaks, or a lakeside cabin. But there is also a long tradition of urban retreats. Who doesn't like the idea of an apartment on the Left Bank of Paris, a tiny riad in Marrakech, or even a pied-à-terre atop a tower in Manhattan?

But you needn't go far to escape the everyday. These clients, who are based in San Francisco, found their ideal escape in Los Angeles, where the husband, a developer, was working on several large projects. When he and his wife came upon a small single-story house in West Hollywood, they immediately saw its potential. The previous owner had doubled the size of the property by purchasing the house next door, tearing it down, and using the land to install a swimming pool and diminutive garden. One of the great charms of the house was that practically every window and door looked out onto greenery, and the accessory dwelling unit at the back helped to create a sheltered patio for entertaining.

OPENING SPREAD: In the great room of a single-story house in West Hollywood that serves as a getaway for a San Francisco couple, side chairs by Jacques Adnet are covered in a Fortuny fabric that resembles camouflage and was inspired by the islands of Venice. The walls are matte white, and the ceiling is painted a similar color; the photographs are *Screened Pictures #31* by Anthony Hernandez, left, and *Paradise* by Katy Gammon. The husband plays the piano every day when they are in residence. PREVIOUS SPREAD: The French doors open to the entry courtyard. The bookcases were adapted from ones owned by friends of Rheinstein, and the games table is a custom design. The photograph, *My Ghost*, is by Adam Fuss. OPPOSITE: The photograph over the fireplace is *Girl from Odessa* by Rineke Dijkstra; the low daybed and slipper chair were inspired by Madeleine Castaing. The painting over the chest is an abstract work by Lisa Oppenheim.

Whereas the couple's primary home in San Francisco is sleek and contemporary, this property would provide a contrast to that aesthetic. While the house had definite appeal, it was dated and worn, and it wasn't immediately clear how to make it work for a couple who are disciplined even in their pleasures. The husband plays classical music on the piano, draws, and runs and swims laps every day. The wife is a dedicated cook. And both are involved in the arts.

With its three pairs of double French doors lining one side of the living room, the structure had something of the feel of New Orleans, where Rheinstein grew up, and she immediately embraced that idea. "Our inspiration was a Creole cottage, but done for today," she says. "We wanted to evoke that mix of old and new, charm but with efficiency." She adds, "It was the architect, Hans Baldauf, who has worked with the developer on several commercial projects, who had the idea of turning most of the ground floor into one large space, a single expansive room for living, dining, and relaxing. We thought of it as a loft space, but a loft within an old Creole cottage. And they were great clients. Not every homeowner will let you transform a two-bedroom house into a one-bedroom."

Establishing a single large space is one thing; making it beautiful and functional is entirely another. Rheinstein's inspiration was to make certain that the single room answered a variety of needs even as it evoked a conglomeration of cultures, with references not only to New Orleans, but also Morocco, and southern Africa, and

PREVIOUS SPREAD: The 1970s dining table by Maison Jansen has a top of reverse-painted glass and is paired with vintage Louis XIV-style chairs. The pendant light was designed by Ted Abramczyk for Ralph Pucci, the photograph is *First Flowers* by Robert Learoyd, and the custom cabinet from Quintus hides a television that rises up when desired. OPPOSITE: Above the fireplace on the opposite side of the room hangs a photograph by Hiroshi Sugimoto of a wax museum figure of Catherine Parr, the last wife of Henry VIII. The chairs are upholstered in an African-inspired printed linen, and the 1960s stacking side tables are covered in Korean newspapers.

ABOVE: The coffee table is a 1940s French design,
reminiscent of the work of Gilbert Poillerat.
RIGHT: The powder room walls are covered in
pewter tea paper to give the tiny space a subtle
shimmer; the sconces and antiqued mirror add to the
effect. OPPOSITE: The marble-topped commode of
mahogany inlaid with mother-of-pearl resembles a
1940s piece but is nineteenth-century Italian. Rather
than a tray, a bronze brazier holds the liquor bottles.

with more than a touch of French 1940s glamour thrown in. A strong dose of up-to-the-moment modernity is provided by the couple's collection of contemporary photography.

Rheinstein began by establishing an envelope of softly textured matte white walls via sheets of "caba" paper applied by hand in vertical stripes around the room, a subtle but potent detail that enriches the experience. The designer contrasted that with a ceiling of glossy beige and her signature painted floors in a geometric pattern so understated as to be almost monochromatic. She then filled the room with outstanding pieces from a variety of eras, all cohabitating peacefully—one of her great strengths as a designer. A low daybed and slipper chair evocative of Madeleine Castaing ("She was one of the inspirations," Rheinstein notes) are placed in front of a limestone mantel, hand carved to evoke snakeskin, at one end of the room, near an early nineteenth-century Italian commode inlaid with mother-of-pearl. The matching fireplace surround at the other end of the room is topped by a Hiroshi Sugimoto photograph of Catherine Parr and flanked by armchairs upholstered in a fabric inspired by Kuba cloth, a 1940s French coffee table, and 1960s stacking tables covered in Korean newspapers. The Maison Jansen dining table has a reverse-painted glass top and is paired with vintage Louis XVI chairs. Above it hangs a contemporary pendant light by Ted Abramczyk from Ralph Pucci.

The antiques are supplemented with custom pieces, including a games table for dominoes and backgammon, the bookcases flanking the French doors to the terrace,

PREVIOUS SPREAD AND OPPOSITE: The kitchen, which leads to the garden and the guesthouse, is fitted out with a custom stove by La Cornue for the wife, who is an avid chef. The leather stools, found at J.F. Chen, were a request from the husband who wanted a place to perch while his wife cooks. The photograph, *Calabasas Pool*, is by Larry Sultan.

The walls and ceiling of the main bedroom are painted in Farrow & Ball's Mizzle, a soft, enveloping shade. The lozenge shapes painted in the same color on the floor subtly enliven the room. The bed hangings are of a printed, textured linen by Madeaux.

which were adapted from a piece owned by dear friends of the designer ("I asked their permission," she says), and a console that hides a television.

The great room gives onto a kitchen fitted out with a La Cornue stove, a special request from the wife, who is a true food connoisseur and loves to entertain, and a pair of 1970s leather upholstered brass stools, a response to the husband's desire for a place to perch while she cooks. (His specialty is mixing cocktails, which is why the bar in the main room is so well stocked.)

The adjacent bedroom is as refined but slightly more sumptuous thanks to its soft textiles. The room is shrouded in what Rheinstein terms "one of those beautiful no-color colors," and fitted out with a pair of original Syrie Maugham chairs found in San Francisco.

If the main house emits a sublime stillness and poetic atmosphere, the accessory dwelling unit, formerly a garage, is exuberant and a bit over-the top, a brash exotic fantasia. "We wanted to evoke a Moroccan casbah, not an authentic one, but everyone's ideal of a 1970s casbah," the designer says jokingly. "Morocco as seen through the lens of the 1970s, a little bit Yves Saint Laurent, a little bit Bill Willis." The main room's walls, ceiling, and low banquettes are covered in a richly detailed paisley fabric. Cabinetry of Moroccan screens backed by mirrors lines one wall, hiding utilities and storage, but most importantly, adding depth and magic to the room. The bedroom beyond sports a trompe l'oeil tented ceiling, creating the effect of sleeping in the desert.

OPPOSITE: Two original Syrie Maugham chairs found in San Francisco and re-covered in the same fabric as the bed flank the bedroom fireplace. The photograph is by Adam Fuss. FOLLOWING SPREAD: The bath features floors of reclaimed marble from Chateau Domingue. To the right of the tub is a photograph of Sinéad O'Connor by Herb Ritts (another bald head by Robert Mapplethorpe is on the other side). The sconces are by Porta Romana.

PREVIOUS SPREAD: In the main room of the guesthouse, which was formerly a garage, the walls and custom banquettes, which are fitted with proper mattresses, are covered in Clarence House paisley fabric. The floor tiles, which appear warm and mellow, were made recently in Los Angeles. The wall lights are from Katie Leede, and the small lacquer tables are from Reed Smythe & Company. The diptych, *Echo*, is by Jim Goldberg. ABOVE: The powder room is sheathed in a Martyn Lawrence Bullard tile wallpaper. A cabinet from Morocco is fitted with a stone top and serves as the vanity. OPPOSITE: A wall of Moroccan treillage over mirror hides storage, a bar, and a television, while visually expanding the space. FOLLOWING SPREAD: The bedroom is sheathed in Rheinstein's Lenare Paisley pattern, and the ceiling is painted to evoke the feel of sleeping under a tent. The lantern is from Soane.

Just outside is the patio, with plantings by Dryden Helgoe Landscape Design, and a large brick fireplace, an outdoor living room sheltered by the main and guesthouses. Beyond, beckons the pool, with a copper-roofed pool pavilion fitted out with a comfortable sofa and chairs. "It gets cool at night in Los Angeles, and you need shelter," the designer says. "And you need shade during the day."

PREVIOUS SPREAD: The garden courtyard, which features plantings designed by Dryden Helgoe and a mix of vintage pieces and furniture by Rose Tarlow and Formations, provides shade during the day and shelter on cool evenings. ABOVE: The upper terrace with a brick walkway from the street to the pool beyond. OPPOSITE: The pool pavilion features a copper roof and a floor of brick. FOLLOWING SPREAD, LEFT: The interior of the pavilion is cooled by a deep blue-green ceiling. The sofa is covered in a Konstantin Kakanias design. RIGHT: At the opposite end of the pool, a Munder Skiles bench is sheltered by tall clipped hedges.

San Francisco

We like to think that we adapt a house to our needs, but just as often, we adjust ourselves to fit a house. Aside from the few who can afford to build a new home that specifically responds to their every desire, most of us learn to accommodate quirky layouts, rooms that are slightly too small, crammed closets, awkward kitchens, low ceilings, or inelegant proportions. We balance our needs with our desires, weighing a great location against a too-small space, a dramatic view against a balky elevator. We compromise, we accept, we stop noticing the annoying little quirks of the places where we live. But then our lives change, our needs evolve, and the balance gets skewed. Suddenly, all the small inconveniences we have put up with for so long that we hardly even notice them, come to the fore.

That was very much the case for the owners of this town house near the Presidio in San Francisco. They had lived in the house for thirty-eight years and loved its gracious rooms and stunning views over the city and the bay. They had raised their daughter in the house and felt a deep connection to their neighborhood and

PREVIOUS PAGE: A circa-1700 William and Mary walnut veneered chest, a pre-Columbian polychrome female figure from the Jana Coaque culture in Ecuador, a betel nut box from Java, a lamp made from an eighteenth-century Italian candlestick, and trompe l'oeil drawings in ink and wash, circa 1592–1630, exemplify the diversity of cultures and periods collected by the owners of a San Francisco town house. OPPOSITE: In the entry, a handmade Adelphi wallpaper, an abstracted stripe bolder than a traditional Georgian pattern, unifies the spaces and sets off an array of heirlooms, including a Spanish console, a California landscape, an important ship painting, and an Oriental rug.

community. But the minor annoyances they had dealt with for decades began to seem not so minor, to the point that they even considered moving.

The couple are world travelers and are involved in the arts, serving on the boards of several important institutions, including the Spoleto Festival. They love to entertain. They are healthy and fit—they think nothing of heading out on arduous hikes over rugged terrain in the Bay Area or spending six weeks trekking in Africa— so the house's four flights of stairs were not a problem. But there were other issues. The wife is an expert cook and haunts the local farmers markets, yet she had never had a truly workable kitchen. They host frequent dinner parties, but once the meal was finished, the living room never really felt like a welcoming place to hang out, so everyone would climb several flights to reach a comfortable spot for after-dinner drinks and conversation. And each time the husband wanted another bottle of wine during dinner, he would have to head to the basement to retrieve it. A two-story 1960s addition at the back of the house overlooking the garden had never been integrated into the flow of the house. And the handsome decor, originally overseen by renowned San Francisco antiquarian Robert Domergue, was looking a bit worse for wear. After more than thirty-eight years, who of us doesn't need a refresh?

The couple ultimately decided to stay, but they knew changes needed to be made. So, they reached out to Rheinstein. "There was never any discussion about a radical makeover," says the designer. "We all wanted to respect the house and its

PREVIOUS SPREAD: A pale gray paper-backed silk with a slight texture on the walls establishes an enveloping atmosphere in the living room. The palette of soft roses, grays, and blues was inspired by the Turkish rug the couple had long owned. The artworks that enrich the room include a bust of Egon Schiele, a fine old tapestry, an important nineteenth-century still life, and a Buddha that they acquired on their travels. OPPOSITE AND FOLLOWING SPREAD: The dining room's traditional table and chairs are set against walls covered in a hand-painted and glazed stripe of deep blues and rose. The room, with its Dutch brass chandelier and formal mantel, takes on a more modern feel thanks to the sisal rug.

architecture. This was decidedly a case where I wanted to do the most with the least." And the house had the advantage of good furnishings and art—it was just that everything was all mixed up. Important paintings that had been in the family for generations were mixed with powerful examples of pre-Columbian objects, Asian art, and other works they had acquired on their world travels. "Pieces were dispersed all over the house, and the rooms had become a bit of a mishmash," says Rheinstein. "The house needed a clarifying eye to showcase the wonderful items and artworks they owned in a more compelling and coherent way."

Clarity was needed for the layout as well. "I wanted to brighten the house, make it more functional, but also more soothing and seductive," she adds, "to reflect the sophistication of the owners and their relaxed and confident approach to the world. I sought to create rooms where their traditional dark-wood furnishings would stand out elegantly against soft backgrounds." The staircase acts as the central spine of the house, and Rheinstein acknowledged its importance with a gutsy custom-colored wallcovering by Adelphi Papers, with the surrounding trim painted a warm gray.

To give a more comfortable flow to the main floor, Rheinstein wanted to clarify the connection between the living and dining rooms. "My primary concern was to make it a space that worked for entertaining," she explains. A pale gray paper-backed silk with a slight texture sheathes the living room walls, creating a warm and soothing atmosphere, and the furniture was installed to make after-dinner relaxation and conversation easy and effortless. In the dining room, the traditional table and chairs stand out against a backdrop of a glaze painted stripe of deep blues and rose. "It is a

OPPOSITE: The powder room vanity is copied from an antique piece that Rheinstein owned and was painted to look like rosewood. The Georgian-style gilt screen on the door gives it a special jewel-box effect. Katherine Jacobus stenciled the walls to look as if they are upholstered in button-tufted fabric.

ABOVE AND OPPOSITE: The new kitchen serves as a transition between the formality of the front of the house, and the more casual double-height space at the back. Cabinets and an island of whitewashed oak are fitted with dark countertops. The industrial metal cabinet over the range is contrasted by a wall of handmade, irregular tiles, produced in the same way as traditional Delft tiles but with no ornamentation. The wicker chairs are upholstered in the traditional way, the pendant light is by Urban Electric, and the stools are by Sawkille.

RIGHT: To brighten the lower level, which opens onto the garden, the rough, dark wood paneling was lime-washed. Furnishings include Moroccan rugs, rattan chairs, a sofa upholstered in Rheinstein's Indian Zag fabric, and a painted burlap coffee table. The drawing over the fireplace is by Fernand Léger, and the rhino hide warrior shields are from a trek the owners made in Africa.

ABOVE: The custom cabinet, inspired by one the designer spotted in the San Francisco store March, is fitted out with subtle lighting to showcase the couple's collection of pre-Columbian artifacts. The door conceals storage, and bookshelves are tucked behind the spiral staircase that rises to the kitchen. OPPOSITE: The interior of the bar cabinet is fitted with pull-out trays for bottles and glasses; the ceramic plaque above it is by Picasso.

pattern you hardly notice at first, yet it envelopes you," she says.

The new kitchen became the fulcrum of the house, serving as a crucial transition between the formality of the front of the house and the more casual double-height space at the back. This was the designer's greatest intervention: "We gutted the kitchen and took advantage of the opportunity to move the spiral staircase to the lower level to the opposite side of the room. We installed new cabinets and an island of whitewashed oak, fitted with my favorite dark countertops." A sleek metal hanging cabinet adds an industrial edge, but it is placed over a wall of handmade off-white tiles, creating a contrast between machine- and hand-made.

The lower level, which opens to the garden, is the most casual and most "California" room in the house. To brighten the space, the designer had the dark paneling lime-washed. She installed hidden storage and crafted a cabinet with subtle lighting to showcase the important pre-Columbian pieces the couple own. "Gathered together here," she says, "they have far more impact than before. And though the couple were initially reluctant, I insisted they install a television in this room, which we placed in a custom étagère."

The powder room became a spot for elegant fantasy, while the bedrooms upstairs were designed as serene retreats. But here again, the old was made new. The primary bedroom's small settee, which is more than twenty years old, was reupholstered since, as Rheinstein points out, "It's the husband's favorite place to read the newspaper each evening." The designer paid special attention to the wife's adjacent study where she plans the duo's trips, fitting it out with Panamanian *molas*,

OPPOSITE: The wife's study on the second floor features a rug found on their travels and a group of *molas*, vivid fabric art appliqués from Panama. The shelves are filled with an array of international souvenirs, African jewelry, handwoven baskets, and other handicrafts acquired on the couple's adventures.

PREVIOUS SPREAD: The walls and ceiling of the expansive main bedroom are painted a soothing green. Much of the room was left as it was originally designed by Robert Domergue years ago, including the dramatic headboard, which was reupholstered. Engraved Venetian mirrors flank it, and the settee at the foot of the bed, the husband's favorite place to read the newspaper, was re-covered in Darby Rose by Jasper. RIGHT: The top floor sitting room has a curved balcony overlooking the Presidio.

From the ground floor to the top of the house, each room has been refreshed and rethought, using and rearranging what the couple already owned, embracing the mix of periods and cultures that reflects their unique approach to the world.

an array of international textiles, African jewelry, handwoven baskets, and other handicrafts that remind her of their travels and help inspire new ones.

Up another flight, the sitting area, with its curved balcony overlooking the Presidio and with views of the bay, was left largely unchanged from the way Robert Domergue had designed it. On the same level, under the eaves, is tucked a serene guest room, which Rheinstein swathed in shades of silvery gray. The adjacent sitting room serves as a private refuge where the couple can retreat *à deux* to enjoy the fireplace together.

From the ground floor to the top of the house, each room has been refreshed and rethought, using and rearranging what the couple already owned, embracing the mix of periods and cultures that reflects their unique approach to the world. They are surrounded by the familiar, by objects they love, but thanks to Rheinstein's deft interventions, everything is highlighted in a fresh way, and the house effortlessly responds to the way they live. The house now fits them better than it ever had before.

OPPOSITE: Tucked under the eaves on the top floor, a guest room in shades of warm, pale gray serves as a serene refuge; the prints are antique, and the cabinet is Japanese.

Bel Air

Every designer knows heartbreak. Next to choreography, interior design may be the most ephemeral of the arts. Death, divorce, and disaster can all intervene. A baby is born, children grow up, a company moves its headquarters, the real estate market crashes or booms, and the next thing you know, the perfect home must be left behind, and all that remains are memories and photographs.

For Rheinstein, one of her greatest disappointments came after one of her greatest successes. Clients had asked her to design their 1920s Tuscan-style villa in Bel Air, and the results—full of elegant gilt Italian furniture, refined details, lush textures, and a subtle, soothing palette—was one of her favorite projects, so much so that she included many images of it in her second book, *Rooms for Living*. She and the client had spent months shopping and sleuthing for unusual pieces at auctions, at flea markets, and at high-end antiquaries and connoisseurs including Richard Shapiro, Philip Stites, and the late John Nelson, gathering the kinds of antiques and decorative items that bring personality and distinction to a home.

OPENING SPREAD: The charming facade of one of the outbuildings on a property in Bel Air belonging to longtime clients of Rheinstein's. This one is used as a guesthouse and office. PREVIOUS SPREAD: The front of the expansive home, with a double-height living room on the far left, the dining room with its matching bowfront window, and the wing containing the family room and a wine-storage room, with bedrooms upstairs. Beyond are garages and other outbuildings. OPPOSITE: A Russian icon in an intricately carved vineyard frame, a fifteenth-century Spanish chest on stand, and a nineteenth-century Italian chair all stand out against the Georgian paneling in the entry. Many of the furnishings were acquired for the clients' previous home.

RIGHT: The mix of styles in the entry hints at the range of Grand Tour treasures within. The sconces and unusual console are eighteenth-century Italian and came from Richard Shapiro, and the chairs are Dutch.

RIGHT: The unusual, oversize candle sconces were part of the decor in the clients' previous house. The chair is Italian, and the new wood floors were stained a rich chocolate brown.

ABOVE: The sconces in the powder room are by American ceramicist Eve Kaplan. OPPOSITE: This contemporary version of a garniture is also by Eve Kaplan and is displayed on an Italian carved walnut console. The stools are also Italian antiques. The painting is by Stephen Edlich.

Then the house was sold, and all those treasures were put into storage. But this story has a happy ending. The couple ultimately located another house in the same neighborhood that more than fulfilled their needs. This one was a 1920s Georgian, which, though smaller than their previous house, occupied an expansive and flat piece of land, ideal for a growing family with members of all ages. There was no question that they would again turn to Rheinstein, who had made their former house such a success. "This was something of a 'puzzle house,'" says the designer, "in that the challenge was getting it all to fit together. The clients had all these beautiful Italian pieces from their previous house, and I was determined to make them work within what was now an English Georgian envelope."

The house, which had been revamped several years before by Ferguson & Shamamian Architects, has rigor but also a sense of relaxed sprawl. In the main house, the living and dining rooms, with matching bay windows, flank the formal entry with its columns, with bedrooms located above. To one side is an expansive wing that contains a family room, kitchen, and wine-tasting space. Just behind it is a separate cottage with a fully fitted-out guest suite, the husband's office, and next to it, the garages. Across the expansive lawn is a pool house and tennis court. The last bit of charm comes via a fanciful striped pavilion tucked behind the guest cottage.

While their previous residence had the feeling of an exquisite old family villa in the Italian countryside, refined and sheltering, the new house is more classic

PREVIOUS SPREAD AND OPPOSITE: In the double-height living room, a back-to-back banquette anchors one end of the room, facing a seventeenth-century velvet-covered bench and a settee in the Portuguese style. The icy blue-green fabric on antique chairs from Richard Shapiro contrasts with the warm beiges and rose tints that predominate in the room. The work over the fireplace is by Frank Stella, and the sisal rug was woven on a kilim loom, which gives it an especially smooth and subtle texture. The French doors lead out to a newly constructed pergola, and the hanging lantern is from Jamb.

OPPOSITE: Accessories throughout gleam and magnify the light, including Victorian silver shells and Italian gilded and painted wooden candlesticks on the mantel. ABOVE: A painted table and a lamp made from an antique fragment. RIGHT: The gilt and glass coffee table by Maison Jansen is topped by an Italian Lacca Povera box.

PREVIOUS SPREAD: The dining room walls are covered in a Fortuny cotton with stripes, some in the subtlest metallic gold. Chairs in a linen damask and the simple silk curtains with bobble fringe were used in the clients' previous house. ABOVE: The art assemblage near the window, titled *Pentimenti*, is composed of rubble taken from the demolition of a historic church, gilded and arranged by the artist Shinji Turner-Yamamoto. OPPOSITE: The mirror glimmers softly, as do the old gilded pieces and even the tabletop.

"My decorating is very object driven," says Rheinstein, "but it's not only about rare and expensive treasures. I also love a beautiful, timeworn basket or an old table of beat-up wood. They can be treasures, too."

American, but on a grand scale, instantly evoking images of lazy summer afternoons or twilight cocktails, summer parties, and long leisurely dinners.

Rheinstein retained the building's baronial touches—the plaster ceiling in the dining room, the classic wood paneling in the entry hall and living room, the severe neoclassical mantels. But the formality is undercut with sensual textures, a pale, almost monochromatic, color scheme, and subtle but striking decorative touches that evoke a sense of relaxed luxury, from the ball fringe on the living room upholstery to the Fortuny fabric in the dining room, with a faint metallic stripe that gleams in candlelight. The rich browns of the various woods stand out as sculptural elements against the pale walls. Disparate eras and continents of origin coexist in surprising harmony. As Rheinstein says, "My decorating is very object driven, but it's not only about rare and expensive treasures. I also love an old basket or a table of beat-up

PREVIOUS SPREAD: Most of the furnishings in the wine-tasting room came from the previous house, including the Italian sacristy cabinet that is lined with Ultrasuede to hold glasses and carafes, an Italian settee, a simple wood table, and the French chairs that retain their original tapestry upholstery. The benches are covered in a cut velvet, and candlesticks by Ted Muehling add a contemporary gleam.
OPPOSITE: Wicker chairs upholstered in gingham contrast with the pantry's existing metal storage unit.

RIGHT: In the primary bedroom, the bed was painted to resemble inlaid ivory, a touch inspired by Frances Elkins. A Bennison silk was used to line the bed hangings and for the curtains. The neoclassical mirror over the mantel is eighteenth century and the porcelain flowers are sculpted by Vladimir Kanevsky.
FOLLOWING SPREAD: In the family room, a work by Richard Diebenkorn, one of a pair, hangs over the slate mantel whose twin is across the room. A collection of seventeenth- and eighteenth-century bronze mortars and vessels are displayed throughout the room.

wood. They're treasures, too." The house gives the immediate impression that it is lived in by world travelers who have filled the rooms with items selected for their intrinsic beauty and charm, and who are only too happy to share their discoveries with family and friends.

As with so much of Rheinstein's work, outdoor areas are crucial, and this expansive property gave her numerous opportunities to conjure relaxing spots in the fresh air. Many of the rooms open to the garden, and under a newly constructed pergola, surrounded by landscaping designed by Lisa Zeder, inviting rattan and 1920s stick wicker furniture beckons, all of it painted a uniform soft blue green. The pool house across the lawn has become a favorite family gathering place, with its billiard table and comfy bobbin chairs.

"It's a very welcoming house," says the designer, who has carefully guided the transition of the family's belongings, setting them to advantage within a new context, refurbishing and reupholstering where necessary, casting a fresh eye on familiar items, seeking out additional treasures when needed. Pulling together this house was never about constraints or making do, but rather taking the opportunity to conjure a new vision using well-loved pieces, which has always been a touchstone of her career. Quality lasts, and Rheinstein proves that again with this home, where the family is ensconced as elegantly and comfortably as ever, surrounded by all the beautiful objects they love and have assembled over the decades.

PREVIOUS SPREAD: The wife's study under the eaves is sheathed in Rheinstein's Woodcut fabric for Lee Jofa, which was inspired by a scrap of Japanese textile. The same fabric covers the club chairs and ottoman, creating a unified, serene, and restful retreat. The lacquered and brass-trimmed desk is by Gracie, the chair is Regency, the rug is sisal, and the works flanking the window are embroidered and appliquéd needlework pictures. OPPOSITE: In the separate guesthouse, the husband's office is grounded by an indoor/outdoor rug designed by Bunny Williams for Dash & Albert. A vintage octagonal table from North Africa and unusual objects from many places are reminders of a life well-traveled.

While their previous residence had the feeling of an exquisite old family villa in the Italian countryside, the new house is more classic American, but on a grand scale, instantly evoking images of lazy summer afternoons or twilight cocktails, summer parties, and long, leisurely dinners.

PREVIOUS SPREAD: The steel bed in the guest room, with hangings of a Peter Dunham fabric, and the long banquette are from the previous house. The collages flanking the bed are by Jean-Charles de Ravenel. OPPOSITE AND FOLLOWING SPREAD: The new pergola off the living room features an outdoor fireplace, making it ideal for gatherings on cool nights. The 1920s stick wicker furniture is painted a uniform pale blue green, the antique tile-top table was custom made, and the Moroccan vases covered in Persian poetry are from Richard Shapiro. Across the lawn is the pool house, which has become another favorite place for family get-togethers.

As with so much of Rheinstein's work, outdoor areas are crucial, and this expansive property gave her numerous opportunities to conjure relaxing spots in the open air. Many of the rooms open to the garden and a newly constructed pergola. The pool house across the lawn has become a favorite family gathering place.

OPPOSITE: The interior of the pool house features a billiards table copied from an eighteenth-century French engraving and an unusual Chinese drum from Richard Shapiro that serves as a coffee table. The shades and curtains of a Robert Kime fabric were adapted from the previous house, and the artwork is a tantric painting by an anonymous artist.

ABOVE: The view of the main house from the pool house. OPPOSITE: The striped metal pavilion, referencing one in Sweden's Haga Park, is tucked behind the guest house and serves as a family gym. FOLLOWING SPREAD: The patio off the family room is shaded by an awning to protect it from the afternoon sun and is fitted out with comfortable furniture by Formations, making it an ideal spot to relax and contemplate the pool and pool house.

Newport Beach

PREVIOUS SPREAD: The
entry hall of a house in
Newport Beach, across from
the bay and a small, sandy
beach. RIGHT: The house was
originally designed by Tichenor
& Thorp, and was modified
by architect Gil Schafer, who
also designed the new building
to the left, which is used for
gatherings and for guests.

Artists tend to retain certain hallmarks throughout their careers. Even as their imagery, styles, and techniques evolve, their work demonstrates their signature in every mark, every brushstroke, every color choice. The best fashion designers, too, will remake classic pieces over decades, updating their signature little black dress, trench coat, or smoking jacket to keep them of the moment, adjusting the fit, the fabrics, and the proportions, but always retaining some indelible element that identifies the piece as their own, without anyone ever needing to inspect the label inside.

The best interior designers, too, have their signatures—the fabrics, colors, furniture shapes, and finishes they opt for time and again. For Rheinstein, these favored elements include painted floors, scenic murals, glossy ceilings, theatrical powder rooms, and luxurious, cossetting bedrooms. But of course, the circumstances, locations, and ways in which these signatures are used always vary, and the results are always distinct. Rarely is a designer brought back to literally reconceive their work of previous decades—and expand on it.

But that is exactly what happened with this house in Newport Beach. Rheinstein had originally designed the house years before, with such success that she featured

OPPOSITE AND FOLLOWING SPREAD: The living room of the main house is painted in Farrow & Ball's Mouse's Back, with the ceiling a glossy version of the same color to reflect the sunlight. It evokes a sandy coastal retreat without resorting to conventional blue and white. The painted tole flowers are by Carmen Almon and the collage to the left is by Kinuko Imai Hoffman. The artwork over the fireplace is an unusually large woodblock print by Helen Frankenthaler, and the sculpture on the table by the banquette is by Larry Mohr.

The living room's palette of pale beiges and grays is enriched by a variety of textures and subtle detailing throughout, including a silk stripe on a painted side chair, one of a pair that belonged to Bunny Mellon (above) and a woven linen on a club chair (right). OPPOSITE: The rich color of the walls makes a wonderful background for the art, here a painting by Elliott Puckette. The custom banquette is upholstered in a variegated ottoman weave.

it in her first book. And the clients were so pleased that they turned to her again to design their house in Sun Valley, Idaho. Now their children were adults, but their family had only expanded over the years with the arrival of grandchildren. Their circle of friends had increased, and they were entertaining much more frequently. Their art collection had also grown significantly. Three years ago, they began looking at other properties in search of an up-to-date house with more space. Then everything changed when the adjacent property came on the market.

"It presented a very special opportunity," the designer recalls. So rather than move, the couple decided to think differently. They would revamp their current home and buy and tear down the structure next door to make room for a new family retreat specially fitted out for entertaining, with extra bedrooms for family and guests.

Their main house had originally been designed by Tichenor & Thorp, but for this venture the couple chose architect Gil Schafer, whom Rheinstein knew from their work together for the Institute of Classical Architecture & Art. The two had even traveled together happily. "Gil changed the front of the house, enlarged the kitchen, rearranged the rooms upstairs, and converted what had been playrooms into a gracious dressing room and closets," she says. He designed the new house next door not to match the current house but to complement it. Both structures are shingled and painted the same shade of white.

PREVIOUS SPREAD AND OPPOSITE: The paneling and floor in the dining room/library were painted by Bob Christian to resemble the bleached wood beloved by Frances Elkins, and the tole-and-crystal chandelier is from the clients' previous house. The wing chairs are upholstered in Rheinstein's Mimi Crewel fabric, the watercolor over the mantel is by Paul Lucien Maze, and the painting by Kinuko Imai Hoffman is from Gerald Bland.

PREVIOUS SPREAD: With its beadboard ceiling, painted floors, and Shaker-inspired cabinetry, the kitchen evokes an elevated country aesthetic. Antique Windsor chairs surround a gateleg table, and the French Directoire pendant light above the island originally hung over a billiard table. RIGHT: In the study, the walls are covered in a woven straw cord, the desk is Continental, the shades are of a Robert Kime print, the sconces are by Visual Comfort, and the vintage ceiling light is from J.F. Chen. The cabinets were finished to resemble cork, and the lamp was made from an old tin storage jar.

ABOVE: The Napoleonic prisoner of war straw-work picture of a ship reads as abstract from a distance.
FOLLOWING SPREAD: The family room off the kitchen is a place to retreat, with enveloping color
and inviting seating. Marian McEvoy was commissioned to create the collaged screen of petals and leaves,
which hides the TV. Over the sofa is a painting by James Nares.

Inside the main house, the designer aimed to simplify but also elevate, acknowledging the house's proximity to the beach, but never forgoing formality completely. The ample rooms, spare layout of the furnishings, limited range of colors, and tactile richness of the details bring a sense of elegance and reserve. "We saved a lot of what was already in the house, but refined the rooms," she says. "We changed the palette to pretty neutrals, with touches of blue throughout."

The living room's glossy ceiling and painted floors amplify the room's abundant light, transforming it into an active presence. "We wanted the ceiling to evoke a sandy beach," the designer says, "while the subtle octagons on the floor bring to mind the seaside without resorting to the more expected blue and white." A clean-lined banquette, a minimal steel coffee table, and artworks by Elliott Puckette and Helen Frankenthaler play off against traditional armchairs sporting loose floral slipcovers and gilded side chairs that once belonged to Bunny Mellon.

With its shelves of multicolored books and pale *faux-bois* finishes by Bob Christian, the dining room/library is more low-key and intimate. The floors had been refinished several years before, but the designer considered them too red, and decided to have them painted as well. And she proudly points to the room's triple-hung windows: "just like Thomas Jefferson had at Monticello," she notes. The chandelier is one of the many pieces retained from the house's original incarnation. "It's tole and crystal, not too grand, so it still works," she says.

The kitchen was revamped with new cabinetry, and the appliances were shifted to create a better workflow. "We wanted it to look like a room that just happens to be a kitchen," says the designer. "The kitchen is central to the layout, because you have to go through it to get to the family room." At the request of the client, Rheinstein selected a variety of putty shades for the room, and over the island,

ABOVE: One of the blue chairs is antique, the other is a copy, after the husband declared it the most comfortable he had ever sat in. The artwork is by Ellsworth Kelly. OPPOSITE: The swing arm lamps are vintage, the artworks are by Lee Krasner (above) and Jean Dubuffet (below), and the vintage rug is from Jamal's Rug Collection.

PREVIOUS SPREAD: Many of the furnishings in
the main bedroom were retained but freshened with
new fabrics and colors. The crewelwork curtains
from Chelsea Editions and the bed linens by Julia B.
came from the previous house. The Italian painted
secretary, just visible, holds a television. ABOVE: The
bedside lamps are 1940s decalcomania, with the images
pressed onto glass from within. RIGHT: The bedroom
showcases a few favorites from the clients' collection
of American embroideries and other pastimes of
women in the eighteenth and nineteenth centuries.

installed a pendant light that originally hung above a billiard table. The breakfast area features antique Windsor chairs and a gateleg table that were among the first, and most prized, antiques the couple had ever acquired. "It opens onto the patio and the covered porch of the new house," she says. "There are lots of citrus trees planted on the grounds, so you get the most wonderful fragrance."

The adjacent family room is a cool retreat in shades of sea green and vivid blues, as in the James Nares artwork and the upholstery of the armchairs, one vintage, the other a copy, because "the husband told me it was the most comfortable chair he had ever sat in." A charming decoupage screen by Marian McEvoy incorporating real leaves and pressed flowers hides the television over the mantel, a replacement for one the designer had found in England, but which was lost in a fire that destroyed her storage space, "one of the great heartbreaks of my career," Rheinstein says.

Upstairs, in the bedrooms and study, restraint holds sway, with many of the favorite items repurposed and showcased in a fresh way via new fabrics and wall colors. "We wanted what they love to shine through," says the designer. "It was important to incorporate the pieces that really had meaning for them."

If the main house is spare and refined, the new structure is more rustic and relaxed, far more colorful, and studded with whimsical touches. "We wanted to make it look like it had been there awhile," Rheinstein says. The two-story house consists of a double-height great room with an open kitchen with vivid blue cabinetry on one side ("Although no one really cooks there," the designer admits. "It's mostly used for warming and serving"), with two cozy bedrooms and baths tucked under the eaves upstairs. The walls of the main floor are paneled in shiplap, immediately establishing a casual, seaside feel. "We obsessed over how rough to make the boards," she says. "And then we had all the walls and the exposed beams lime-washed." Custom banquettes

OPPOSITE: A bed by Michael S. Smith in a guest room is upholstered in a Lee Jofa hand-blocked linen, used on the wrong side to give a softer effect. The lamps are of opaline glass, and the needlepoint rug is by Vermilion. ABOVE: The bathroom sconces are vintage.

ABOVE: In another guest bath, the tub and floors were painted *faux-marbe* by Mimi Feldman. The Victorian shellwork picture above was once owned by Tony Duquette. OPPOSITE: The guest room bed is upholstered in a hand-printed pattern from Raoul Textiles.

If the main house is spare and refined, the new party and guesthouse is more rustic and far more colorful, studded with whimsical touches. "We wanted to make it look like it had been there awhile," Rheinstein says.

mix with vintage rattan chairs, an oversize sofa, old copper lanterns, a Napoleon III chair, a Calder braided-hemp tapestry, and an original Syrie Maugham sofa, "though the husband joked that it would soon become a Syrie Grand-mum sofa." Subtle patterned fabrics add a vivacious feel to the room, amplified by touches of vivid blue. The bedrooms and baths upstairs are not large but are thoughtfully fitted out, enlivened by striped and sprigged wallcoverings and fabrics.

The covered porch off the kitchen serves as the link to the main house, where it abuts the patio and rear entrance. With its plush, vintage stick-ware seating and outdoor fireplace, the porch has become a favorite spot to gather for cocktails, conversation, and cigars. "The wife told me she knew the guesthouse was a success when, on the morning after big game nights, she would find the topiary pots full of cigar ashes," the designer says with a laugh.

OPPOSITE: The new guesthouse was designed to complement the main house but has a more rustic and relaxed atmosphere. The back entry off the porch contains a sideboard painted by Jon Jacobs that serves as a bar; the vessel is a nineteenth-century pickling jar. FOLLOWING SPREAD: In the double-height great room, vintage rattan chairs mix with Napoleon III chairs and other comfortable seating, a vintage Swedish column cabinet, and custom rugs. The walls are covered in lime-washed, slightly rough sawn boards.

PREVIOUS SPREAD: The oversize sofa and curtains are in two different weights of linen printed in the same pattern by Douglas Funkhouser for Le Gracieux. Under the window is a Syrie Maugham–style sofa from Jonas. OPPOSITE AND ABOVE: Custom banquettes covered in a Foley & Cox fabric flank the entry. The swing arm lamps are by Gregorius Pineo, the small tables are powder-coated metal, the Napoleon III club chairs from J.F. Chen are covered in a modern linen print with linen fringe, the Turkish chair is by Jonas, and artworks, opposite, are by Bridget Riley (above) and Paul Kremer (below), and, above, by Sam Messenger.

ABOVE: A lamp made of cork pieces by Marian McEvoy stands on a Portuguese table in front of a braided-hemp tapestry by Alexander Calder. The mirror over the mantel hides a television. OPPOSITE: The artworks over the table are by Joan Michell (above) and Elliott Puckette (below), and the large painting is by Sarah Graham.

OPPOSITE: The small kitchen's open shelves and brightly stained cabinetry add to the casual feel of the guesthouse. The photos are by Adam Fuss—the client had purchased one and then inherited another from the same series from his mother—and the lights are by Robert Kime. ABOVE: A wallpaper by Robert Kime and antique ship paintings and "woolies," images crafted by sailors, line the staircase; the lantern is antique and adds to the atmosphere of the new guesthouse.

PREVIOUS SPREAD: The bedrooms upstairs under the eaves were designed to be simple and cozy. The bed is upholstered in the same embroidered fabric that covers the walls and ceiling. The Italian side tables, which are finished on all sides, were turned to fit in the intimate space. OPPOSITE: The second guest room is sheathed in a striped paper. The twin beds and the rug, which was designed to look early American, are custom designs. ABOVE AND RIGHT: The baths feature vanities with unlacquered brass fittings by Lefroy Brooks. The dressing room closet was inspired by one John Stefanidis installed in a Scottish hunting lodge. FOLLOWING SPREAD: The covered outdoor porch serves as a link between the two parts of the building—the great room and the guest rooms—and makes a cozy refuge on cool nights. The furniture is mostly 1920s stick wicker, and the fireplace surround is of old stone, to add to the comfortable, relaxed feel.

Montecito

With her love of beautiful objects—whether rare Georgian furniture, humble woven baskets, aged garden urns, Italian painted furniture, or contemporary tole flowers—not to mention her passion for plush velvets, faded chintzes, printed linens, and intricate paisleys and ikats, it would be hard to consider Suzanne Rheinstein a minimalist. Such was her passion for finding and sharing beauty that her store, Hollyhock, was for decades one of Los Angeles's most prestigious design emporiums, and its wares, ranging from unique vintage finds to works by contemporary artisans, were incorporated into a shockingly high percentage of the city's most stunning homes.

And yet Rheinstein's rooms never overwhelm. Quite the contrary. Increasingly over the years, the spaces she creates have become ever more spare and serene. In her rooms, atmosphere and light take precedence, time slows down, contemplation comes naturally, and beauty is allowed space to breathe. Each item is considered, set off to its best effect, but the totality is far more powerful than any single element.

PREVIOUS SPREADS: The entry and facade of Suzanne Rheinstein's retreat in Montecito. The house was originally built in the early 1970s and was revamped by the designer with architects Richard Bories and James Shearron to create a simple, low-slung structure where the volumes, textures, and natural light would predominate. New whitewashed stone walls enclose the entry in the gravel forecourt, and the mature Metrosideros tree and Roman pines on the property were retained. OPPOSITE: In the entry, Spanish colonial cooking pots on stands are placed atop a seventeenth-century Portuguese table. The Etruscan wine urn came from Tom Stansbury Antiques, and the composite torso, a fragment of what was once an Italian figural grouping, was found at Karla Katz Antiques in New Orleans. The floors throughout are pale oak.

This is true for every project in this book, yet there is no better exemplar of her ability to conjure supremely refined relaxation than her own getaway in Montecito.

Rheinstein had long been hoping to find a house in the area, but the desire became even more intense after an accident in the fall of 2013 shattered her foot and elbow and left her immobile for months. "I was in the hospital, coming out of surgery, when I saw photographs of the place, and a floor plan," she says. "The house hit the market on a Friday, and that Sunday I put in a bid without even seeing it."

What attracted her was neither the design of the house, which had been built in 1971, nor its condition, which she frankly describes as "in pretty horrible shape," but the property itself, and the setting. "The place has fantastic views of the Santa Ynez mountains. It was sad and overgrown, but there was a huge backyard with a circular pool—perfect for senior synchronized swimming," she says, joking.

For help, she turned to the team of Richard Bories and James Shearron, whose work she admired, and who had worked with her daughter, Kate. The architects retained the footprint of the house, but totally transformed its look, managing to find within its 1970s Fire Island aesthetic the ghost of a more appropriate form, echoing the early Spanish vernacular intrinsic to Montecito. Now the pale stucco-clad forms seem to hug the landscape, as clean-lined and strong as a modernist sculpture.

Because this was an entirely personal project, Rheinstein could adapt the interior to her desires and needs, ignoring conventions. So, there is no dining room: "One thing I knew for sure about this house is that I wouldn't be giving any formal

OPPOSITE AND FOLLOWING SPREAD: The walls inside and out are covered in a hand-applied integrally colored plaster. The living room walls change color throughout the day and are hung with a group of pochoirs from the Antipolis series by Picasso. The light fixture is by Giancarlo Valle, the table is from Gerald Bland, and the English Regency chairs are painted *en grisaille*. The slipper chairs are upholstered in a Carolina Irving stripe with hemp fringe, and the chaise longue is eighteenth-century French in the Louis XIII style.

OPPOSITE: A drawing of an enlarged epiphyte by Sarah Graham hangs over a Portuguese library table with distinctive baluster legs. The sofa is inspired by one in the Palazzo Mariano Fortuny, and the bronze-and-lacquer coffee table is Rheinstein's design, crafted by Quintus. ABOVE: In a corner of the living room, a Tuscan table holds a group of ceramic pots and hyacinths by Kaori Tatebayashi. Above it hangs a work on paper with punctures, *Concerto Spaziale,* by Lucio Fontana; the stools are Swedish.

ABOVE: The Romanesque stone lions looking in from the garden are from the Puglia region and date to the twelfth through the thirteenth century. OPPOSITE: The antique stone sink in the powder room was one of the first pieces Rheinstein bought for the house. The sink and fittings are from Compas, the antique mirror is Portuguese, and the sconces are by Paul Ferrante.

dinners," she says with a laugh. But there is an expansive flower arranging room off the garden. What had been the guest room became her primary bedroom: "So now I can lie in bed and see the mountains." The kitchen chairs are all on wheels because her three granddaughters love to scoot around on them.

The living room contains her signature mix of eras and origins, with boldly sculptural Portuguese furniture mixing with antique Italian mirrors, African spears, Etruscan wine vessels, plush, pale upholstery, and modern art by Pablo Picasso and Lucio Fontana. The den is fitted out with a custom banquette perfect for lounging, and the first television she has ever had mounted over the fireplace. "It's where I spend time alone in the winter," she says, and considers the room her "cabinet of curiosities," fitted out with Giorgio Morandi prints, Japanese brush pots, and architectural fragments from India.

What had been the dining room became the reading room, centered by a raised mattress she calls her "Princess and the Pea bed," where she loves to sprawl with her granddaughters, who share her love of reading. The wall over the fireplace is adorned with plates from Robert Kime, faded, mottled, and adorned with encrustations after having spent a century or more under the ocean after the ship that was transporting them sank.

Each detail is considered, with color and texture as important as shape. The monochromatic plaster walls are the color of palest sand, which seems to change throughout the day as the sun moves across the sky and clouds drift in and out. The

OPPOSITE: In the reading room, low bookcases flank stacked mattresses covered in Rheinstein's Indian Zag fabric. The plates over the fireplace, from Robert Kime, were rescued from a sunken ship. Once blue and white, they now feature beautiful encrustations from being buried at sea for two hundred years. The chairs are vintage rattan, and the artworks include a Picasso pochoir and ink drawings by Dug Uyesaka, left, and a painting by Kinuko Imai Hoffman, right.

ABOVE AND OPPOSITE: The reading room looks out onto the pool and garden. The eighteenth-century Italian faux-painted storage columns were found in New Orleans. Nepalese iron cooking pots hold foliage from the trees outside. The painted chair is English Regency.

furnishings and objects all stand out strongly against the simple planes and barely-there color. That prominence justified her in indulging in hand-cast brass hardware and iron latches from van Cronenburg, a foundry in Ghent, Belgium. Though she is no snob, and happily incorporated light fixtures from Pottery Barn and accessories from RH: "I always say, go Rolex or go Timex. It's the middle of the road that's the kiss of death."

As with all her projects, the outside was as important as any of the rooms within, so Rheinstein enlisted the help of her old friend Nancy Goslee Power, a renowned garden designer based in Santa Monica. The circular pool was replaced with an elegant rectangular lap pool set off with, on one side, yellow-painted wicker lounge chairs on an expanse of gravel, and lush perennial beds enclosed by a hedge of Japanese blueberry on the other. Every room opens to the outdoors. A pergola topped by a screen of bamboo softens the abundant sunlight, with an outdoor fireplace and custom banquette at one end, where Rheinstein spends many evenings.

William Morris famously said, "Have nothing in your house that you do not know to be useful, or believe to be beautiful." Rheinstein's house in Montecito is such a success because here each item fits both criteria. Like a Matisse cutout or a late Joan Mitchell drawing, the place stands as a distillation of her art, evidence of her hard-won knowledge of who she is, what she loves, and how she wants to live. It is a very personal work by a master who had nothing to prove, no one to please but herself, and only the joy of her creativity to express.

OPPOSITE: In the kitchen, the pendant light came from a 1960s restaurant, via Richard Shapiro's gimlet eye, and was powder-coated the same color as the walls. The table is by Sawkille, and the works over it by Richard Smith were found at J.F. Chen. The island of smooth basalt stone contrasts with the roughly textured paneling behind it.

RIGHT: The den, the only room that is painted (in Farrow & Ball's Mouse's Back) is cozy for watching television on a set designed by Yves Béhar. It is fitted out with a custom banquette with mattresses that can also serve for extra guests. The inlaid Moroccan table is from Indigo Seas, and the painting is by Kinuko Imai Hoffman.

'TE AND ABOVE: Rheinstein considers the den her "cabinet of curiosities" and has filled
    vith I___ian architectural fragments, Japanese brush pots, and contemporary ceramics by
            __ from the Giorgio Morandi estate, and the chair is French.

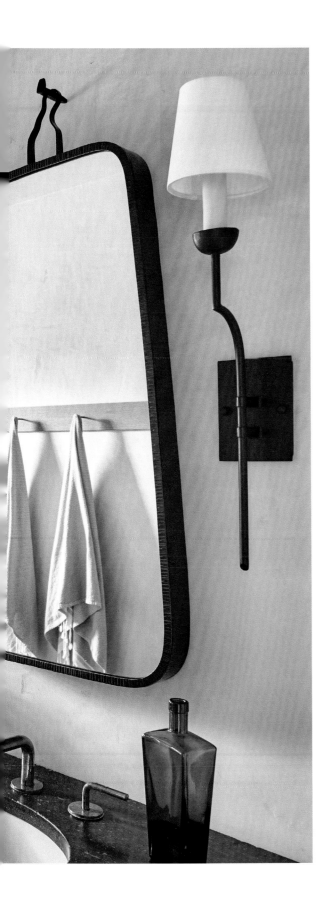

LEFT: In the bath, the shower is lined with zellige tiles from Morocco. The sconces are by Paul Ferrante, and the contemporary mirror was found online.

Distilled Wisdom

• Fewer things, but better ones. Buy one good object a year— whether it's an antique table or a contemporary ceramic vase or a worn, early wicker chair with great lines. In ten years, you will have a strong collection of pieces that will add character to your rooms.

• Once you have assembled a personal collection of one-of-a-kind pieces of furniture and objects, you can shift your rooms from neutrals to brights, from minimally arranged to chock-full o' furniture, and on and on, without ever losing your distinct personality and point of view.

• Consider appropriateness. Try to truly understand how you actually live each day, and how you aim to use your new or revamped rooms.

• Let details reveal themselves over time. Not every room, object, color, or fabric needs to shout "wow." If a room is inviting and comfortable, you will spend more time there, and as the days go by, you will continue to discover great delights.

• Make sure some rooms have a sense of calm—so important with everyone leading such busy lives.

• Curation is as important as choice. How things are put together is crucial. A myriad of nationalities and periods is often more interesting. But sometimes, you need to gather like with like and showcase them all together.

OPPOSITE: The flower arranging room is fitted out with custom oak cabinetry, a granite sink, and a zinc countertop. The pendant light is from Lars Bolander. The room is the last stop on the way out to the garden, so hats, clippers, and totes are all at hand.

• As a design force, texture is undervalued. Go for rough against smooth, nubby handwoven fabrics, velvets, plaster, sisal and straw, shiny lacquer, and worn and waxed woods.

• Always remember that comfort is key. Whether a room is minimalist and neutral or jam-packed and full of color, the same needs apply. Always make sure to have good lighting for reading and conversations, small tables at hand for drinks, a layout that permits easy maneuverability, and generous spaces between pieces.

• Light in a room comes not just from windows and lamps. So many materials can amplify and beautify light—mirrors (I love them aged), gilt accessories, lacquer, and bronze.

• Painted floors enrich and brighten a room, especially in pale colors and simple geometric patterns.

• Broaden your approach to accessories. Unusual objects can be used in unexpected ways. Regency hot water urns become vases, braziers serve as bar trays, Asian lacquered boxes on stands can act as small tables. There's no need to settle for the ordinary when something unexpected can add real interest.

• Outdoor spaces should have the comfort, ease, and beauty of those indoors, with inviting seating, pillows, sturdy tables, candlelight lanterns, and plants in beautiful containers.

• Go Rolex or go Timex. Both offer excellent value. Going down the middle is the kiss of death.

OPPOSITE: In the passage leading to the main bedroom, a "corkiage" mirror commissioned from Marian McEvoy hangs over a seventeenth-century English Jacobean chest with its original base. The hardware throughout the house is by van Cronenburg, hand forged in Belgium.

RIGHT: In the primary bedroom, a steel bed, originally designed for and sold at Hollyhock, is dressed in the palest blush-colored glazed linen from Rose Tarlow. The settee and ottoman are covered in a hand-blocked linen used on the wrong side. The faux-stone columns and painted cabinet are Swedish, the console in front of the window is quirky Peruvian, via Italian cabinetmakers, and the 1930s tufted chairs are from J.F. Chen.

240

ABOVE: A 1930s wrought-iron daybed in the private garden off the primary bedroom.
OPPOSITE: The painted cabinet in the bath is Swedish, and the side table is a bronze casting
of a Louis XV table.

RIGHT: The guest bed is upholstered in a Rosa Bernal fabric and is flanked by antique Italian painted cabinets. The Continental tapestry and the Italian settee are from Tom Stansbury Antiques.

244

ABOVE: A head of carved tufa from southern Italy, which Rheinstein refers to as her "Sicilian sage," is backed by a hedge of rosemary. OPPOSITE: The pergola is shaded by a roof of bamboo and quick-growing honeysuckle. The chairs are vintage rattan.

OPPOSITE: The outdoor fireplace makes this corner an ideal spot to gather on cool evenings. The built-in banquette is a wonderful place to read or look out at the Santa Ynez mountains. ABOVE: The antique Italian stone fountain head with an iron star was found by Rheinstein years ago, knowing that one day it would find its perfect place. FOLLOWING PAGES: The garden was designed by Nancy Goslee Power, inspired by the work of Spanish garden designer Álvaro de la Rosa and the lush plantings of Dutch designer Piet Oudolf. A hedge of Japanese blueberry barely contains an overflowing bed of Matilija poppies, salvia mexicana 'Limelight', verbena, plumbago, geranium 'Rozanne', and numerous other plants. The lounge chairs are from Anthropologie.

Some Favorite Resources

SHOPS AND SHOWROOMS

There are two shops in California that I love to visit at the beginning of a project, knowing that the unusual pieces I find there will trigger inspiration. Although their inventory is quite varied and different from each other, each proprietor has wide-ranging interests and an extraordinary knowledge of every piece—even the most esoteric treasure.

J.F. Chen, in Los Angeles, is housed in a series of cool spaces that contain his mid-century and many more collections: jfchen.com

Tom Stansbury Antiques, in Newport Beach, sells fine European antiques and collectibles. He also has a by-appointment designer showroom of more antiques and oddities: tomstansburyantiques.com

I adore the showroom and the taste of Gerald Bland in New York. There are several paintings in this book by Kinuko Imai Hoffman, whom the showroom represents, as well as outstanding ceramic objects by Eve Kaplan. The steel furniture Bland designs and produces makes an elegant counterpoint to fine antiques and other kinds of furniture: geraldbland.com

In Santa Barbara, a trip to William Laman is a must. He and Bruce Gregga run their shop from a cottage that is chic and contemporary yet charming, beautifully arranged with a mixture of garden antiques, contemporary furniture and objects, and an array of irresistible accessories and small tables: williamlaman.com

Within walking distance of William Laman is Davis & Taft, owned by Leanne Baker. She has a constantly changing collection of objects and art, especially artists who were active in Southern California at mid-century. I have many drawings and paintings from her inventory, and most of the slightly eccentric 1970s Italian lighting in my own house came from her shop: davisandtaft.com

New York dealer James Sansum is always a great source for elegant and unexpected furniture and refined decorative accessories: jamessansum.com

ARCHITECTS

It is always a delight to work with talented architects, and I had that pleasure on several of these projects.

Ferguson & Shamamian Architects were involved in renovating both the house in Northern California and the Bel Air house: fergusonshamamian.com

The architect of record for the Northern California house was Andrew Mann Architecture: andrewmannarchitecture.com

My own house in Montecito was a collaboration with Bories & Shearron Architecture: boriesandshearron.com

Gil Schafer was behind the renovation of the Newport Beach house and the design of its new guesthouse: gpschafer.com

The ideas of Hans Baldauf were crucial to the success of the West Hollywood getaway: bcvarch.com

The architects for the renovation of the San Francisco town house were Sutro Architects: sutroarchitects.com

LANDSCAPE AND GARDEN DESIGNERS

Creating beautiful, welcoming, and comfortable outdoor spaces is critical to the success of any of my projects, but especially those in California. I was fortunate to work with these exceptional talents:

Nancy Goslee Power
nancypower.com

Dryden Helgoe
drydenhelgoe.com

Lisa Zeder
lzdesigngroupinc.com

Kathryn Herman
kathrynhermandesign.com

Elizabeth Everdell
everdellgardendesign.com

DECORATIVE ARTISTS

What an experience it is to work with Bob Christian—he gets any reference and has terrific ideas of his own to add to the designer's. We have collaborated on many projects and working with him on the Northern California house was a special pleasure:
bobchristiandecorativeart.com

Katherine Jacobus painted the custom-colored glazed stripes on the walls of the dining room of the San Francisco town house, as well as the "tufted buttons" of the powder room:
katherinejacobus.com

Mimi Feldman of Demar Feldman Studios painted the subtle floors in the West Hollywood retreat and helped turn the former garage into a Moroccan fantasia:
miriam-feldman.com

HOME STORES

Beautifully curated home stores, full of surprising finds, quirky furnishings, and enchanting accessories are increasingly hard to find. Two of the best are my daughter Kate's shop KRB, in Manhattan, and in Nashville, Reed Smythe & Company, owned by my friend Keith Meacham:

KRB
krbnyc.com

Reed Smythe & Company
reedsmythe.com

Acknowledgments

To Alexander Paladin, for helping keep the many parts of my life on track, including the making of this book.

To Meredy Vranich, Catherine Sidon, and Priscilla Wright, my longtime collaborators in design, and to Laura Pugh and Heather Christensen, for their unending support. Together we had the SRA design studio humming with delight.

To the talented people who made this book happen—Pieter Estersohn, whose photographs captured the magic of the rooms, and Michael Boodro, whose prose elucidated my thoughts about my wonderful clients and their houses. To Sandra Gilbert Freidus, my editor, and Charles Miers, the publisher of Rizzoli, for their continuing support. To Doug Turshen, who, with David Huang, has designed all of my books for Rizzoli and with whom I am most pleased.

And especially to my clients who are among the most interesting people I know. Thank you for trusting SRA to collaborate with you on making your houses truly "yours."

First published in the United States of America in 2023 by
Rizzoli International Publications, Inc.
300 Park Avenue South
New York, NY 10010
www.rizzoliusa.com

Publisher: Charles Miers
Editor: Sandra Gilbert Freidus
Editorial Assistance: Kelli Rae Patton, Hilary Ney, and Rachel Selekman
Design: Doug Turshen with David Huang
Design Assistance: Olivia Russin
Production Manager: Alyn Evans
Managing Editor: Lynn Scrabis

Printed in China

2023 2024 2025 2026 / 10 9 8 7 6 5 4 3 2

ISBN: 978-0-8478-9902-9
Library of Congress Control Number: 2022947570

Visit us online:
Facebook.com/RizzoliNewYork
instagram.com/rizzolibooks
twitter.com/Rizzoli_Books
pinterest.com/rizzolibooks
youtube.com/user/RizzoliNY
issuu.com/Rizzoli